Promise

God Is for Us

The Lutheran Spirituality Series

William M. Cwirla

CONCORDIA PUBLISHING HOUSE · SAINT LOUIS

3558 S. Jefferson Ave., St. Louis, MO 63118-3968
1-800-325-3040 • www.cph.org

Written by William M. Cwirla

Edited by Robert C. Baker

This publication may be available in braille, in large print, or on cassette tape for the visually impaired. Please allow 8 to 12 weeks for delivery. Write to Lutheran Blind Mission, 7550 Watson Rd., St. Louis, MO 63119-4409; call toll-free 1-888-215-2455; or visit the Web site: www.blindmission.org.

Manufactured in the United States of America

1 2 3 4 5 6 7 8 9 10 16 15 14 13 12 11 10 09 08 07

Contents

Hymnal Key

LSB=Lutheran Service Book
ELH=Evangelical Lutheran Hymnary
CW=Christian Worship
LW=Lutheran Worship
LBW=Lutheran Book of Worship
TLH=The Lutheran Hymnal

About This Series

In the West, spirituality is as nebulous as it is popular. Having succumbed to humanism, rationalism, and Darwinism, communities once known for a genuine Christian piety now provide a fertile breeding ground for self-made theologies, Eastern religions, the worship of science and technology, or even a resuscitation of the old pagan gods. In a highly competitive environment, each of these spiritual philosophies seeks to fill the vacuum left by the seemingly departed Christian spirit.

Even among faithful Christians, and at other times and places, spirituality has run the gamut from the mystical to the almost sterile. From the emotional to the pragmatic, the experiential to the cerebral, the all-too-human desire to experience (and control!) the divine has proven to be especially resilient. Influenced by modernism, postmodernism, and whatever comes next, even those who try faithfully to follow Jesus Christ may find defining *spirituality*, or at least what is distinctively Christian about their own beliefs and practices, a significant challenge.

Do Lutheran Christians have a spirituality? Indeed they do! This adult Bible study series explores the rich depths of a distinctively Lutheran spirituality that begins in Baptism and is founded upon God's Word. There, the incarnate, crucified, and resurrected Lord proclaims His victory over sin, death, and the devil, and from there flows the proclamation of His Gospel and the administration of His Sacraments. It is through these means presented within the liturgy of His Church that Christ communicates not merely spiritual energies, an emotional high, a method of reasoning, or a stringent morality, but truly Himself—God in human flesh.

Written by respected Lutheran scholars in the United States and Australia, this adult Bible study series emphasizes the Bible, Luther's catechism, and the Lutheran hymnal as concrete and integral resources for a truly Lutheran spirituality. May God richly bless those who study His Word, and through His Word may they experience the genuinely enlightening and life-giving spirituality found only in the life, death, and resurrection of our Lord and Savior, Jesus Christ.

The Editor

Participant Introduction

The Lord is a promise maker and a promise keeper. The Bible records God's first promise in Genesis in which He promises to crush the head of the serpent-deceiver (Genesis 3:15). It also records His last promise in Revelation, in which the crucified, risen, and reigning Christ promises, "Surely I am coming soon" (Revelation 22:20). The Bible is the written record of God's promise making and promise keeping.

The life of faith is lived trusting in God's promises, which all find their "yes" and "amen" in Jesus Christ (2 Corinthians 1:20). Faith clings to God's promises and calls upon them in every facet of life. A genuine Christian spirituality, that is, a life shaped by the Holy Spirit working through the Word, is centered and focused on God's promises in Jesus Christ. These promises are worked out in His death on the cross, His resurrection from the dead, and His ascension to the right hand of the Father. Christian spirituality is a trinitarian spirituality flowing from the Father through the Son by the Holy Spirit, from God to us, and returning from us to God.

In our consumer-oriented society, God's promises are obscured by promises of an easy life filled with material abundance, abundant health, and self-centered peace. The emphasis of much of modern Christian spirituality is the promise of the self-actualized individual whose private relationship with God provides an insider's advantage for victorious, purpose-filled living. The spirituality of the Scriptures is quite the opposite. The Christian disciple is called each day to lose one's life, to take up one's cross, and to follow Jesus in the way of death and resurrection. This may seem counterintuitive to today's notion of spirituality, but the spiritual life lived in, with, and under God's promises is lived outside of one's self—in Christ by faith and in the neighbor by love.

This study will explore God's promises for us with a particular emphasis on how these play out in our daily lives of prayer and vocation.

To prepare for "God Keeps His Promises," read Acts 13:16–48.

God Keeps His Promises

My eyes are awake before the watches of the night, that I may meditate on Your promise.

Psalm 119:148

Promises, promises. We make them all the time; we also break them more often than we'd care to admit. Husbands and wives promise to live together "until death us do part." Baptismal sponsors and parents promise that the newly baptized infant will be taught the faith into which he or she has been baptized. Children promise to be home on time or to do better in school. Employers promise raises and benefits to their employees, who, in turn, promise to work hard. Our trust in promises affects our actions and attitudes toward those making and breaking their promises to us.

1. Recall some of the major promises you have made and others have made to you. Were they kept or broken? How did their being kept or broken affect your actions and attitudes toward others?

We Have God's Word on It

2. Read Genesis 3:14–15. This is often called the "first Gospel" in the Scriptures. What promise is contained in God's threat to the devil? How did God ultimately keep this promise in Jesus Christ? What evidence do you see in this passage to indicate that Adam trusted God's promise?

3. Read Genesis 9:8–17. What promise did God make with Noah and the creation? What was the visible sign of this promise? How did and does God keep this promise in Christ?

4. Read Genesis 15:9–21; 17:1–27. What promises did God make to Abraham? What was the result of Abraham's trust in God's promises (15:6)? What was the visible sign of these promises? How are these promises ultimately fulfilled in Jesus?

5. Read 2 Samuel 7:5–16. What promises did God make to David through the prophet Nathan? How were these promises fulfilled in David's son Solomon? How were these promises ultimately fulfilled in David's Son, Jesus?

6. Read Isaiah 25:6–8. What promises does the Lord make concerning Zion and salvation? What assurance does Isaiah offer that this promise will be kept?

7. Read Jeremiah 31:31–34. What promises does God make in

this "new covenant"? How are these promises fulfilled in Jesus Christ?

Just as He Promised

The conception and birth of Jesus marked the fulfillment of God's promises to Old Testament Israel concerning the long-promised Messiah. Over and over, the evangelists, particularly Matthew and John, emphasize that these things happened "in order to fulfill the Scriptures." Of particular note are the New Testament psalms in which God's faithfulness is the basis of prayer and praise. Zechariah's Benedictus and Mary's Magnificat are two such psalms.

8. Read Luke 1:6–79. What promises of God from the Old Testament does Zechariah recall at the birth of his son, John? Try to identify as many as possible. How will John himself be a promise of someone even greater to come?

9. Read Luke 1:46–55. What promises of God does Mary recall in her Magnificat? Compare Mary's song with the song of Hannah (1 Samuel 2:1–10). How are these two women evidence of God's faithfulness to His promises?

Fulfilled in Jesus

The Good News of Jesus is the news of God's promises kept. God promised salvation through Israel, and God made good on His promise in the sending of His Son, Jesus, the Messiah, whose death atoned for the sin of the world and whose resurrection provided the hard evidence that God's Word is sure.

10. Read Acts 13:16–48. This sermon of Paul in the synagogue of Pisidian Antioch gives a dramatic overview of God's promises to Israel and their fulfillment in Jesus. What are the major Old Testament people and events mentioned by Paul? What Old Testament Scriptures does he cite? What role does the bodily resurrection of Jesus have in the promises of God and their fulfillment?

11. Read 2 Corinthians 1:18–22. Discuss how every promise God has made is answered "Yes" in Jesus Christ. The word *amen* means "it is sure." Why is it appropriate that we say our "amens" through Jesus Christ, our Lord? Discuss this statement: Jesus is God's promise incarnate.

Spiritual Exercises

- Recall the promises of God you have learned and discussed in this section, and apply them to your own life as a baptized believer. You may wish to write down your insights in a notebook or journal.
- Pray meditatively on the promises of God. Luther taught a simple fourfold way of prayer that begins with a text. Begin with the Scriptures you have studied in this session. Reflect on one or several passages that particularly struck you. First, tell God what you learned about His promises. Second, confess how those promises have not had their way with you and how you have not always trusted them. Third, ask God to deepen and widen your knowledge and trust in His promises. Fourth, thank God for fulfilling His every promise to you in Jesus.
- Each day during the coming week, sing or say the hymn "I

Know My Faith Is Founded" (*LSB* 587; *ELH* 494; *CW* 403; *LW* 354; *TLH* 381).

Point to Remember

For all the promises of God find their Yes in Him. That is why it is through Him that we utter our Amen to God for His glory. (2 Corinthians 1:20)

To prepare for "Children of the Promise," read Galatians 4:21–31.

Children of the Promise

Let Your steadfast love come to me, O LORD, Your salvation according to Your promise.

Psalm 119:41

Children live on promises, and they trust wholeheartedly that promises made to them will be kept. The father who promises a toy to his child will be sure to hear, "Dad, you promised." No wonder Jesus compared the life of faith to that of a little child! Faith clings to God's promises. The promise of forgiveness, life, and salvation in the death and resurrection of Jesus creates and enlivens this childlike faith. As baptized believers, we are truly "children of the promise."

12. Try to recall some of the major promises that shaped your childhood and growing up. What place did promises have in your family, in your congregation, in civil society? What would life be like if there were no promises?

God's Last Laugh

13. Read Genesis 18:1–15. What was the promise God made to Abraham and Sarah? What was Sarah's reaction to God's promise? Read Genesis 21:1–7. How did God keep this promise? Why is Isaac's name appropriate?

14. Read Genesis 16:1–15; 21:8–21. How did Abraham not trust God's promise? What promise did God make to Hagar and her son?

Of Abraham's two sons, Ishmael and Isaac, which one could properly be called the "son of the promise"?

15. Read Ruth 1:1–22. What promise did Ruth make to her mother-in-law Naomi (see vv. 16–18)? Compare Ruth 4:18–22 with Matthew 1:5. What place does Ruth, the Moabite, have in God's promise of salvation through the Messiah of Israel?

16. Read Matthew 1:1–16. In what way could this list be called the "children of the promise"? Take special note of the women mentioned in Matthew's genealogy: Tamar (Genesis 38), Rahab (Joshua 2), Ruth, and Uriah's wife (2 Samuel 11–12). What do you learn about God's promise from the presence of these women in the genealogy of Jesus?

17. Read Romans 8:12–17. How do we know that we are the adopted children of God? Read Romans 9:6–9. Who are the true children of Abraham and "children of the promise"? What makes a true Israelite?

18. Read Galatians 4:21–31. Who are the "children of the slave woman" in this analogy? Who are the "children of the free woman"? Who is "our mother" in Holy Baptism?

Children of God

Children are conceived and born. That may seem obvious, but it needs to be said. The Father has only one Child, namely the "only-begotten" Son. All His other children are those who are born "anew" and "from above." The baptized believer is a "child of God" because he or she is in Christ, God's Son. As children of God in Christ, baptized believers receive all the promises of the "sons of God."

19. Read John 1:10–13. To whom does God give the right to be called "children of God"? This passage lists three ways we are *not* children and one way that we *are*. What are the three ways we are *not* born the children of God? What is the one way we *are* born the children of God? Read John 3:5–9. How and through whom does this birth take place?

20. Read Galatians 3:26–29. In Baptism every person is treated exactly the same whether circumcised or uncircumcised, slave or free, male or female. What does this tell you about the gift of salvation and the inheritance of eternal life? What two gifts of being baptized into Christ are identified in this passage? In what way are women properly "sons of God" according to this passage?

A New Identity

Children draw their primary identity from their family, especially their father, mother, and siblings. As children of God baptized believers draw their identity from their heavenly Father, and their brother, Jesus the Son, and the Holy Spirit, their guardian and guide. When children act contrary to their family identity, fathers are quick to point out, "That's not who you are!" Baptism gives us a new identity in Christ Jesus as children of God. Sin is no longer who we are; that belongs to old, dead Adam. Who we are is determined by who God says we are, namely His children (1 John 3:1).

21. Read 1 Corinthians 6:9–11. Some of the Corinthians apparently had quite a past. But their former sins do not define their present identity. Their past is what they *were*, but not who they *are*. How does Paul indicate the present identity of the Corinthians? What is their future as a result? What does this mean for you as a baptized believer?

22. Read Ephesians 5:1–20. What does the life of a "dearly beloved child of God" look like according to this passage? Contrast the "children of light" with the "sons of disobedience." What place does repentance and forgiveness of sins have in the life of a child of God?

Spiritual Exercises

- Your fellow members are brothers and sisters through Holy Baptism. Write down some of the special needs of your baptismal brothers and sisters of which you are aware, and try to fulfill one or two of them each week. It may be something as simple as a phone call or visit or sharing a meal with someone who is alone.
- Pray the Third Article of the Creed together with its meaning from the Small Catechism.
- Each day this week, say or sing the hymn "God's Own Child, I Gladly Say It" (*LSB* 594; *ELH* 246). Take some time to meditate on each of the stanzas by saying them out loud and remembering that they apply to you in your Baptism.

Point to Remember

See what kind of love the Father has given to us, that we should be called children of God; and so we are. The reason why the world does not know us is that it did not know Him. (1 John 3:1)

To prepare for "The Promise of Baptism," read Romans 6:1–10.

The Promise of Baptism

We must think this way about Baptism and make it profitable for ourselves. So when our sins and conscience oppress us, we strengthen ourselves and take comfort and say, "Nevertheless, I am baptized. And if I am baptized, it is promised to me that I shall be saved and have eternal life, both in soul and body."

Large Catechism, Part IV, paragraph 44

"Nevertheless, I am baptized!" was Luther's retort to the accusations of sin and conscience. This is the promise of God trusted in faith and put to use. We sometimes hear people speak of the promises we make in Baptism. The real promises in Baptism are made by God to us. Here, all that Christ accomplished by His incarnation, His perfect life, His sacrificial death on the cross, His resurrection and ascension are revealed, offered, and applied to us personally in the name of God. To be baptized is to have the personal assurance of the triune God Himself that we are His children. With God's testimony comes many wonderful promises—sure as God's name is sure.

23. How might Luther's dictum, "Nevertheless, I am baptized!" be a source of aid and comfort to you? How you use this to help someone you know who might be weak or wavering in the faith?

Through Water and Spirit

24. Read Genesis 1:1–3. What role did water and the Spirit have in the creation of life?

25. Read Genesis 6:1–8:22. How was the flood a re-creation of the creation? How was the flood a kind of death and resurrection for

Noah, his family, and the animals? On what day in Noah's life was the ark opened again (8:13)? Read 1 Peter 3:18–22. How is the flood a picture (type) of Baptism? What promise does Peter draw from Baptism?

26. Read Exodus 13:17–14:31. How is the crossing of the Red Sea a picture (type) of Baptism? Can you find the Spirit of God at work in this narrative? In what way was the crossing of the Sea a kind of birth for the nation of Israel?

27. Read 2 Kings 5:1–15. Some early Church Fathers saw Naaman's healing in the Jordan River as an Old Testament allusion to Baptism? How did God heal Naaman of his leprosy? How did this miracle serve as a sort of rebirth for Naaman (see vv. 14–15)?

28. Read Matthew 3:13–17. What did the Father say at Jesus' Baptism? What did the Holy Spirit do? According to Jesus, why was it necessary for Him to be baptized?

29. Read Matthew 28:16–20. How are the apostles to "make disciples of all nations"? What promise does Jesus make to them in this disciple-making activity?

For You and for Your Children

In Baptism, God's promises fulfilled in Jesus are made our own in a personal way. Every person is baptized individually, by name. On the cross, God saved the world and all of humanity in the death of Jesus, His Son. In Baptism, God saves a particular person and calls him or her to be His own child of His promise. From the time of the apostles, children were baptized because they, too, were included in the promise of salvation. In fact, you might say that adults are baptized as though they were children. Regardless of age, everyone is born anew from above (John 3:3) in the water of Baptism.

30. Read Acts 2:37–39. What promises does Peter preach regarding Baptism? To whom do these promises apply? Read Acts 16:25–33. To whom did Paul apply the promise of salvation in Jesus, and whom did he baptize in Philippi? Discuss this statement: It is contrary to the Gospel to refuse Baptism to infants and young children.

31. Read Romans 6:1–10. What does Baptism do according to this passage? In light of what Paul says here, why would it be desirable to baptize a child a soon as possible?

The Promises Overflow

Baptism is like a deep, underground aquifer that springs up and overflows with promises and blessings. One of our problems is that we aren't aware of all that God does in Baptism. Another problem is that we fail to draw on Baptism. It's like having a large bank account but never drawing any money from it, living as though we were poor. The baptismal font brings promises overflowing.

32. Read Mark 16:16; 1 Corinthians 12:3; Galatians 3:27; Colossians 2:12; 1 Peter 3:21; and Titus 3:5. List the gifts and promises of Baptism according to these passages.

33. Read 2 Corinthians 1:20–22; Ephesians 1:13; and 4:30. The word *seal* refers to a mark of ownership put on a person or an animal. What blessings and promises does the seal of Baptism convey? In this light, read Revelation 7:1–8. How does the seal of Baptism protect us against the coming judgment?

Spiritual Exercises

- If you don't know the date of your Baptism, try to find out. The congregation in which you were baptized should have a record of it. If you can't find the date of your Baptism, pick a day to serve as your honorary baptismal day.
- Pray the Small Catechism on Holy Baptism. Say each of the four parts aloud and concentrate on the words. Thank God for the water and Spirit that have given you a new birth and life in Jesus.
- Sing or speak the hymn "All Christians Who Have Been Baptized" (*LSB* 596).

Point to Remember

We were buried therefore with Him by baptism into death, in order that, just as Christ was raised from the dead by the glory of the Father, we too might walk in newness of life. (Romans 6:4)

To prepare for "The Promise of Absolution," read John 20:19–23.

The Promise of Absolution

But we should hold in high and great esteem God's Word in the Absolution part of Confession. We should not proceed as if we intended to perform and offer Him a splendid work, but simply to accept and receive something from Him.

When I urge you to go to Confession, I am doing nothing else than urging you to be a Christian.

A Brief Exhortation to Confession, paragraphs 18 and 32

Baptism is but once in a lifetime. Just as we are born once, so we are reborn once. Yet Baptism has daily impact and promises. We are clothed with Christ's righteousness and are covered with His forgiveness. Sin, guilt, and shame make it easy for us to forget who we are as God's children. We may fall into despair and doubt—even doubting that we are truly saved in Christ. Even though we receive Baptism once in our lives, the gifts of Baptism are renewed every time we hear the Word of God forgiving our sins. Just as we were washed with water and the Word in Baptism (Ephesians 5:26), so in Holy Absolution we are washed with the Word of forgiveness, returning us again to the promises God made to us in the water of Holy Baptism. Forgiveness frees us from the past to live freely in the pres-ent with the promise of a bright future.

34. Think of times when you have intentionally forgiven someone or you have been forgiven by someone. How did forgiveness enable you to move forward in your relationship with that person? How does guilt and shame imprison and isolate us in our own sin? How does forgiveness provide release for both the forgiver and the one forgiving?

A Cleansing Word

35. Read 2 Samuel 12:1–14. How was David's sentence against the rich man in the parable a sentence against himself? What were God's accusations against David? What was David's confession? How was David forgiven? What does the death of David's son teach us about God's temporal discipline and His forgiveness?

36. Read 2 Samuel 12:15–25. What significance is there to the fact that David's son died on the seventh day of his life? How does David express his faith in the promise of God? How does God show Himself faithful to His promises?

37. Read John 20:19–23. Why were the disciples meeting behind locked doors? What does Jesus say and do to bring peace to their hearts? How does Jesus authorize them to forgive sins? What does this teach us about Holy Absolution as we hear it in church today?

38. Read Matthew 18:15–18. How are we to deal with those who have sinned against us? At what point are we to involve others and why? At what point does the Church get involved and why? What is the promise of God given to the Church in verse 18? Discuss this sentence from Luther: "The Church is a mouth-house of forgiveness."

39. Read Psalm 32. This is one of the seven penitential psalms that deal with the personal side of confession and forgiveness. What physical effects did the psalmist feel as the result of his silence regarding his sin? What was the result of his confessing his sin? Read James 5:13–17. Does it surprise you to see Confession and Absolution as part of the pastoral care of the sick?

40. Read 2 Corinthians 2:5–11. At what point does a congregation need to reach out in forgiveness to one who is under discipline? Why is it important that forgiveness be the ultimate goal in the congregation's dealings with its members?

Joy Restored

Unconfessed sin is like a festering wound. The infection spreads from the original site and gradually affects the whole body. It holds the sinner captive in a prison of secrecy. Absolution provides the healing balm of the Gospel on the specific place where sin has done its damage. Specific forgiveness spoken to specific sins breaks the cycle of secrecy and floods the wound with the healing blood of Jesus.

41. Read Psalm 51:1–6. In this passage, against whom does David say he has sinned (v. 4)? Why is it important that all sins be seen as sins against God? How deep does David say his sinfulness goes (v. 5)? Do we sin because we are sinful, or are we sinful because we sin?

42. Read Psalm 51:7–19. What does David want God to do for him (list as many actions as possible)? What does David fear (v. 11)?

What does David desire (v. 12)? What are some of the ways the sin robs you of the joy of your salvation? What is the result when David is freed from his sin (v. 13)? How are vv. 16–17 and v. 19 reconciled with each other?

An Embassy of Reconciliation

The apostle Paul calls his ministry a "ministry of reconciliation," and he sees himself as an "ambassador of Christ" (2 Corinthians 5:18, 20). That makes the Church an embassy of reconciliation where the Prince of Peace brings a peace that surpasses our understanding by His own dying and rising. As an embassy of peace, the Christian congregation both hears and speaks peace.

43. Read 2 Corinthians 5:16–21. What is true of someone who is "in Christ"? How can you be certain that you are "in Christ"? What did God accomplish in the death of Christ (v. 19)? Luther referred to v. 21 as a "sweep swap" or "happy exchange." What is exchanged according to this verse? How does this verse enable us to disown our sin so that we no longer identify with it?

44. Read Matthew 18:21–35. Are there any practical limits to forgiveness? Compare the debts of the two servants in the parable. How does the debt of our sins before God compare with the debt of those who have sinned against us? How does this parable apply to the Christian congregation and to the individual believer?

Spiritual Exercises

- Meditate prayerfully on the penitential psalms (Psalms 6; 32; 38; 51; 102; 130; and 143). Look for the blessings and promises of forgiveness in these psalms. Sing or speak the hymn " 'As Surely as I Live,' God Said" (*LSB* 614; *ELH* 417; *CW* 308; *LW* 235; *TLH* 331).
- If your conscience is troubling you, make arrangements with your pastor to use private Confession. There is a simple order of confession drawn from the Small Catechism in *Lutheran Service Book*, pp. 292–93. Use the Ten Commandments as a template for your confession.
- Intentionally seek the forgiveness of someone against whom you have sinned—a family member, a congregation member, a friend, a co-worker. Intentionally seek to forgive someone who has sinned against you.

Point to Remember

Blessed is the one whose transgression is forgiven, whose sin is covered. (Psalm 32:1)

To prepare for "The Promise of the Lord's Supper," read 1 Corinthians 11:17–32.

The Promise of the Lord's Supper

Therefore, the Sacrament is given as a daily pasture and sustenance, that faith may refresh and strengthen itself [Psalm 23:1–3] so that it will not fall back in such a battle, but become ever stronger and stronger.

Large Catechism, Part V, paragraph 24

The Lord's Supper is a meal filled with promise—the promise of forgiveness, life, and salvation. Jesus established this Supper of His body and blood on the very night He was betrayed unto death, literally on the same day He gave His body and blood as an atoning sacrifice for the life of the world. In this holy Supper, as in Baptism and Absolution, God's promises fulfilled in Christ are made personally our own. God speaks them to us as we hear the words of Jesus "given and shed for you" and we receive with our own mouths the gifts of Jesus' sacrifice on the cross—His body and blood.

45. What are some of the things you remember most about receiving the Lord's Supper? How does receiving the body and blood of Christ on Sunday provide strength and sustenance for your life of faith throughout the week?

Eating and Drinking with God

46. Read Exodus 12:17–28. How did the Passover meal unite every Israelite with the event of the exodus? How did the children of the family learn about the exodus? In what ways is the Passover a picture or type of the Lord's Supper?

47. Read Exodus 24:1–11. What did Moses do with the sacrificial blood, and what did he say? How might this event at Sinai be considered a type of Word and Sacrament event? What is the special gift of this event in vv. 10–11? How does the Lord's Supper fulfill the same for us today?

48. Read 1 Kings 19:1–9. What miraculous food did God provide through an angel? Read verse 7 again. How might this verse also apply to us in regards to the Lord's Supper?

49. Read John 6:51–59. What promises does Jesus make to whoever "feeds on My flesh and drinks My blood"? In verse 52, the Jews in the Capernaum synagogue asked, "How can this man give us His flesh to eat?" How would you answer them in view of the Lord's Supper?

50. Read Matthew 26:17–30; Mark 14:12–26; and Luke 22:14–38. Compare each of these accounts of Jesus' institution of the Lord's Supper. How are they similar? What is the unique gift of each account?

51. Read 1 Corinthians 11:23–26. How does Paul's account compare with the accounts from the Gospels? In what ways does this account clarify the ongoing use of the Lord's Supper in the Church?

How long does the apostle Paul say that the Lord's Supper is to continue?

The Breaking of the Bread

From the very beginning of the New Testament Church, the Lord's Supper was a central element of Christian worship. This should not be surprising to anyone familiar with the Scriptures. Table fellowship with God is a major theme throughout the Old and New Testaments. Jesus Himself taught and ate with people constantly. On two occasions, He fed large crowds with multiplied bread and fish. Two incidents in particular profoundly shaped Christian worship and liturgy and illustrate how central the Lord's Supper is in Christian spirituality.

52. Read Luke 24:13–35. How is this episode on the road to Emmaus similar to the Divine Service? What does Jesus say is the main point of the Scriptures? What place did the "breaking of the bread" have in this story? How might this be instructive to us about the place of the Lord's Supper in the life of the Church?

53. Read Acts 2:42–47. Describe life in the first Christian congregation to emerge from the events of Pentecost. What activities characterized their gatherings? Do you see the early outline of the liturgy in v. 42?

One Bread, One Body

The promise of forgiveness of sins in the Lord's Supper is also a promise of life and salvation. In eating the one bread, the body of Christ, we are the body of Christ. You might say that the Church is what she eats! This unity in the body of Christ means that we are in communion not only with God but also with our fellow baptized believers in a "communion of saints"—holy things uniting a holy people. Here is a community that can be found nowhere else on earth, a community that mystically includes "the angels, archangels, and all the company of heaven." Holy Communion always happens with "peripheral vision"—with eyes fixed on Jesus and His gifts to us, in view of our fellow baptized believers with whom we are "one body" in Christ.

54. Read 1 Corinthians 10:14–17. In what way is the Lord's Supper a Sacrament of our unity with Christ? In what way is it a Sacrament of our unity with one another in Christ? Why is it important that we commune with our fellow baptized believers in view as we receive together the body and blood of the Lord?

55. Read 1 Corinthians 11:17–33. In what ways were the Corinthians dishonoring the body of Christ? What was the result? How might this have been avoided? Why is a greeting of peace among congregation members within the Divine Service an appropriate gesture? In Luther's 1526 post-Communion prayer, we pray that Christ's body and blood would work "faith toward Thee and fervent love toward one another." How is this prayer consistent with this reading from 1 Corinthians 11?

Spiritual Exercises

- Make self-examination a regular, intentional part of your preparation to receive the Lord's Supper. Read Luther's "Christian Questions with Their Answers" (see *LSB*, pp. 329–30).

- Pray the Small Catechism on the Lord's Supper. Acknowledge the gift of Christ's body and blood as food and drink together with the blessings and benefits that go with the Sacrament.
- Meditate prayerfully on the New Testament psalm, the *Nunc dimittis* (Luke 2:29–32). Consider it both in light of a post-Communion hymn and a hymn in the hour of one's death. Speak or sing the hymn "O Lord, We Praise Thee" (*LSB* 617; *ELH* 327; *CW* 317; *LW* 238; *LBW* 215; *TLH* 313).
- In the next week, visit someone who is alone, whether at home, in the hospital, or in a nursing home. Offer to accompany your pastor on a shut-in call and bring the comfort of your presence to another member of the body of Christ.

Point to Remember

For as often as you eat this bread and drink this cup, you proclaim the Lord's death until He comes. (1 Corinthians 11:26)

To prepare for "The Promise of Life," read John 15:1–17.

The Promise of Life

Where there is forgiveness of sins, there is also life and salvation.

Small Catechism

"Get a life." You've likely heard that line at one time or another. Perhaps you've said it yourself, or someone has said it to you. The great news of Jesus is that in Him you already have a life! Here is the "secret" of the spiritual life: It is not centered in you but in Jesus Christ who is your life. The promise of eternal life is not simply a promise of life in heaven one day, it is a promise of eternal life here and now. God gave you new life in your Baptism, a life that is renewed in the forgiveness of your sins, a life that flows from Jesus to you in the Supper of His body and blood, a life that is lived now by faith in the Son of God who loved you and gave Himself up for you. As we live in Christ by faith and He lives in us, we discover a life we cannot have any other way. Jesus said, "I came that they may have life and have it abundantly" (John 10:10).

56. How do you view eternal life? How does the promise of eternal life shape your day-to-day living? When you think of the word *life*, what images come to mind?

Abundant Life

57. Read John 10:1–18. What do we learn about the promise of life from the image of Jesus as our Good Shepherd? Read Psalm 23. List the good things the Good Shepherd does. How are these realized today in the lives of baptized believers? Of what does the abundant life of the believer consist?

58. Read John 15:1–8. What is the connection between Jesus and the believer in this passage? What does the Father do to make the believer even more fruitful? What do you think this pruning entails? What is the promise in verse 7? What are the conditions of this promise? How might the image of vine and branches be applied to the Lord's Supper?

59. Read Matthew 6:25–34. What lessons can we learn by observing how God cares for His creatures? Of what value are we to God? Instead of worrying, what are we to seek? How might worry or anxiety rob us of the joy of being God's children in Christ? Read Philippians 4:4–9. What does the apostle Paul say we should do in times of anxiety? What does it mean to pray "with thanksgiving"? What is the promise in this passage?

60. Read John 14:15–21 and 16:5–15. What promises come with the gift of the Holy Spirit? What is the work of the Holy Spirit according to these passages? Read again John 16:14–15. What do you think is included in this promise that the Spirit will take from the Son and deliver what is taken to the believer?

61. Read John 17:20–25. For whom is Jesus praying? For what does He pray? How is knowing that Jesus prays for us a source of strength and comfort?

62. Read Luke 23:40–43. As death approached, what prayer did the thief make to Jesus? What promise did Jesus make to him? How does Jesus' promise to a dying criminal comfort us as we consider our own life and death?

Now Heard, Not Yet Seen

Perhaps the greatest "mystery" of the Christian life of promise is that we have already died, risen, and now reign with Christ even as we live out our lives. While this may seem confusing, it follows a consistent pattern. God never does things in bits and pieces. He gives us the whole lot in Jesus—then He gives a whole lot more. Now we are the children of God, and there is still more to come. The abundant life of promise is living in the promise, knowing that when God speaks it is done and that in Christ a promise made is a promise kept by God. Now we must hear and trust; soon we will see.

63. Read Ephesians 1:3–14. Count the number of times the apostle Paul uses the phrase "in Christ" or "in Him." Which is more accurate to say: "We are blessed by God," or "We are blessed by God in Christ"? What are all the spiritual blessings we have "in Christ"? What is the "mystery of God's will" that is fulfilled in Christ? Read Ephesians 1:11–14. When were you included in Christ? What mark of ownership did the Holy Spirit place on you (v. 13)?

64. Read Hebrews 11:1–40. What is the definition of faith according to v. 1? How do the saints of the Old Testament provide examples of faith? What lessons can we learn from these heroes of the faith about the abundant life of faith in Christ?

God's Last Promise and His First

The Bible begins and ends with a promise. Most people don't think of the Book of Revelation as a book of promises, but it is. It is God's last word on His promises. Revelation was written at a time of great struggle and persecution for the Church, especially the congregations of Asia Minor. Things seemed to be going from bad to worse, and many believers despaired that what they believed might not come to pass. Revelation provides an image book of promises kept, the crucified Lamb lives and reigns, His city comes down from heaven as a bride on her wedding day, and her saints and martyrs are eternally blessed—just as Jesus promised.

65. Read Revelation 2:1–3:2. The seven churches of Asia Minor form a kind of cross section of the Church throughout the ages. What are the various promises that Christ makes to His churches in these letters?

66. Read Revelation 22:1–5. How is the image of the river of the water of life a picture of the Holy Trinity? How is it a picture of Holy Baptism? What are the promises of life in this passage? What place and purpose does the tree of life have in this picture of heaven? How does this vision complement the first promise made in Genesis 3:15? Read Revelation 22:20–21. What is the last promise recorded in the Scriptures? What is the Church's faithful response to this promise?

Spiritual Exercises

- Meditate prayerfully on Psalm 27. Note especially the promises of God and the psalmist's trust in God's Word of promise. Speak or sing the hymn "O God, O Lord of Heaven and Earth" (*LSB* 834; *CW* 400; *LW* 319; *LBW* 319).
- For each day of the week, pray one petition of the Lord's Prayer according to the Small Catechism.

- This week, intentionally seek opportunities to speak of life in Christ to another person. Begin with a fellow believer in your congregation, if you wish, and then speak to someone who does not know of God's love in Christ.

Point to Remember

I have been crucified with Christ. It is no longer I who live, but Christ who lives in me. And the life I now live in the flesh I live by faith in the Son of God, who loved me and gave Himself for me. (Galatians 2:20)

Leader Guide

Leaders, please note the different abilities of your Bible study participants. Some will easily find the many passages listed in this study. Others will struggle to find even the "easy" passages. To help everyone participate, team up members of the class. For example, if a question asks you to look up several passages, assign one passage to one group, the second to another, and so on. Divide up the work. Let participants present the different answers they discover.

Each topic is divided into four easy-to-use sections.

Focus introduces participants to key concepts that will be discovered in the session.

Inform guides participants into Scripture to uncover biblical truth.

Connect enables participants to apply that which is learned in Scripture to their lives.

Vision provides participants with practical suggestions for extending the theme of the lesson outside the classroom and into the world.

God Keeps His Promises

Objectives

By the power of the Holy Spirit working through God's Word, participants will (1) remember the promises God made through Israel and how they are fulfilled in Jesus Christ; (2) see the New Testament fulfillment of God's promises in Christ through the eyes of the evangelists and the prophets; (3) recognize that all of God's promises find their "yes" and "amen" in Jesus; and (4) give thanks to God that He keeps His promises to us and grants faith that we might live in the confidence of God's promises kept in Jesus.

Opening Worship

Holy and most gracious God, Your promises are always sure in Your Son, Jesus Christ, our Lord. Grant that we may learn of Your promises to us in Jesus, trust them with a living and lively faith, and with patience and hope look toward their fulfillment; through Jesus Christ, our Lord. Amen.

Psalm: Psalm 18

Sing "I Know My Faith Is Founded" (*LSB* 587; *ELH* 494; *CW* 403; *LW* 354; *TLH* 381).

Focus

1. Answers will vary. Participants are encouraged to explore the various ways promises function in their lives at home, in the workplace, and in church. Examples are wedding vows, contracts, covenants, promises of parents to children, promises made at Baptism or at confirmation or when joining a congregation, and so on.

We Have God's Word on It (Inform)

2. The "first Gospel" (proto-evangelium) is actually a threat to the devil that God would work enmity between the devil and the woman where then there was an alliance. Ultimately, Jesus Christ,

born of a woman, came to crush the devil by His own death on the cross. Adam apparently trusted the promise because even under the sentence of death he named his wife "Eve," which is the Hebrew word for "life," for she would become the mother of all the living. Adam trusted that he would live even though he was sentenced to die. Eve likewise believed, as she said at the birth of her firstborn son, "I have given birth to a man, the Lord," thinking that she had conceived the Promise.

3. God promised that He would never again destroy the whole earth with water. (The next time it will be fire!—2 Peter 3:7, 12.) The visible sign of the promise to creation was the rainbow, appropriate since it is water that refracts the light of the sun into the colors of the prism. The means of destruction (water) becomes the sign of salvation (rainbow). The promise to Noah was kept in Christ by the Baptism that joins us to His death and resurrection. In Baptism, water drowns the old nature but gives birth to the new person in Christ.

4. God promised that Abraham would be the father of many, that his offspring would inherit the land, and that through his promised Seed all nations of the earth would be blessed. Abraham believed God's promise, and God credited Abraham's faith as righteousness before Him. In Christ, the promised Offspring and Seed of Abraham, Abraham has many children who share his faith, and we inherit, literally, an entire, re-created universe along with eternal life with God. Through Jesus, the Son of Abraham, all nations of the world are blessed through His death and resurrection.

5. Through Nathan, God promises David that he would have a son to succeed him who would establish his throne and kingdom and build a house for the Lord's name. Solomon did indeed establish David's kingdom and build the temple in Jerusalem. Jesus, David's greater Son, established David's throne forever at the right hand of God and made His own flesh God's eternal temple, the dwelling place of God with man (see John 2:21).

6. Isaiah depicts salvation on the "mountain of the Lord" (Zion) as a feast of fatted meats and fine wines, similar to the "marriage supper of the Lamb." Feasting and table fellowship with God is a major theme in the Scriptures. The shroud of death will be lifted, and the tears of grief will be wiped away. The assurance for this is the Word of the Lord—"the LORD has spoken." When God says something, it is as good as done. As a funeral text, this reminds those who grieve that God has the last word over death. In His Son, Jesus, and the

mountain of His cross, He has once and for all rolled up the shroud of death.

7. Through Jeremiah, God promises a new covenant in which God Himself will write His Torah (Word) on the hearts and minds of the people who would all know God and that He willforgive and forget their sins. Jesus brings the new covenant with His own blood ("this cup is the new covenant in My blood" [1 Corinthians 11:25]) and by His death takes up our sins so that they are forgiven and forgotten, buried in His death. He also sends the Holy Spirit to renew our hearts and minds and keep them with Christ, revealing Him to us and granting us faith in Him so that we might "know Him."

Just as He Promised (Connect)

8. Zechariah recounts the promises of God at the circumcision and naming of his son, John. God has raised up a "horn of salvation" in this child, promising salvation, mercy based on God's covenant to Abraham, deliverance from enemies, and freedom to serve without fear. The child John will be a prophet of the Most High God, called to prepare the way of the Lord, and will teach the people of salvation through repentance and the forgiveness of sins. John's coming fulfills the promise of the messenger who prepares the way for the coming of the Lord (see Malachi 3:1; 4:5).

9. Mary's and Hannah's songs run in parallel. Both women are bearing extraordinary children of promise. Both speak of God's undeserved goodness and of the great reversal of fortunes by which the humbled are exalted and the exalted are humbled. Hannah's song in particular is noted for this: "The LORD kills and makes alive; He brings down to Sheol and raises up" (1 Samuel 2:6). The extraordinary pregnancies of both these women bear witness to the fact that with God nothing is impossible and that God keeps His promises.

Fulfilled in Jesus (Vision)

10. In almost one breath, Paul takes the hearers in the synagogue through a recitation of what would have been familiar material for them: Israel, the exodus, Samuel, Saul, David, and Abraham. The bodily resurrection of Jesus is held up as evidence that God keeps His Word. Thus, the promise spoken to David, who died and was buried, was fulfilled in the Son of David who rose from the dead. This is a key point in the New Testament: if Christ wasn't raised from the

dead, there is no reason to trust in God's promises (see 1 Corinthians 15).

11. The Father always deals with us through His Son, Jesus, in whom all of God's promises ever made find their fullest expression and fulfillment. Since Jesus is the fulfillment of God's promises, it is proper to speak of the certainty of trust "through Jesus Christ," recognizing that only in Christ are we able to say our "amen" to God. Jesus is God's promise incarnate in that, by His coming in the flesh and entering our history in order to redeem it, all the promises that God had in mind from all eternity are brought to bear on us. Through the same flesh of Jesus, God fulfills His promise of salvation to us in Holy Baptism, the Lord's Supper, and the spoken Word of forgiveness.

Children of the Promise

Objectives

By the power of the Holy Spirit working through God's Word, participants will (1) recognize that in their Baptism they have been made children of God's promise; (2) realize that as children of the promise they have a great inheritance in Christ; (3) discover and embrace their new identity, which is theirs through their new birth from above in Holy Baptism and sustained by the Word and Sacrament; and (4) live in the freedom and confidence of being children of the promise.

Opening Worship

Gracious God, our heavenly Father, by Your great goodness and mercy in Christ Jesus, Your Son, You have made us your children in Holy Baptism and have given us the promise of life everlasting and an inheritance in Christ's eternal kingdom. Grant that we would walk in the freedom of being your children, reflect Your goodness and mercy in the world, and embrace our new identity in Christ; through Jesus Christ our Lord. Amen.

Psalm: Psalm 1
Sing "God's Own Child, I Gladly Say It" (*LSB* 594; *ELH* 246)

Focus

12. Answers will vary. Participants are encouraged to discuss their experiences with promises that were pivotal to their childhood. Be sensitive, because some experiences may have been hurtful. Promises provide a sense of hope for the future. Think of the way a child looks forward to a birthday or to a promised Christmas present. Promises give us a reason to get up in the morning.

God's Last Laugh (Inform)

13. The Lord promised that Sarah would have a son within a year. Sarah, overhearing the conversation from the entrance to the tent, laughed audibly and then denied laughing. A year later, Sarah did indeed conceive and bear a son just as God had promised. His name, *Isaac*, means "he laughs," reflecting Sarah's doubting laughter and God's last laugh. Of Abraham's two sons, Isaac is the son of the promise since he was conceived and born according to the promise of God. Ishmael, though Abraham's lawful son and firstborn, was not the son of the promise since he was born out of Abraham's unbelief.

14. Abraham (Abram) listened to his wife, Sarah (Sarai), instead of the promise of God and had a child by Sarai's maidservant, Hagar. After Hagar and Ishmael had been driven off, the angel of the Lord (Christ pre-incarnate most likely) promised that He would make Ishmael into a great nation; Ishmael would also live as a nomad in hostility against all his brothers (Genesis 16:12).

15. Ruth promised to live as an Israelite under Yahweh, the God of Israel, even though she was from Moab, a traditional enemy of Israel. Ruth's place in the promise of salvation is being the great-grandmother of David. Matthew seems to underscore this in his genealogy of Jesus by specifically naming Ruth in addition to Boaz. This is one of many examples in Scripture of God's universal promise of mercy in Jesus extending outside the boundaries to the "outsider."

16. The genealogy of Jesus is patterned after the lists of Genesis, indicating that God's promise is carried forward through the birth of the promised child. This is often a colorful story, as the presence of the four exceptional women in Jesus' genealogy indicate. Tamar conceived by her father-in-law Judah while posing as a prostitute. Rahab, a prostitute in the city of Jericho, nevertheless trusted the promise of God and was saved from destruction. Ruth was an "outsider" to Israel, a Moabite. Bathsheba is not named, but is called "the wife of Uriah," reminding us of David's adultery and murder. These four women, each in their own way, remind us that God's promise of grace in Christ is unmerited grace toward sinners and extends to all. God works His promise "in, with, and under" the ordinary flow of history, which is riddled with sin.

17. We know we are the children of God because the Spirit of God testifies with our spirit and enables us to say, "Abba, Father." The true children of Abraham are those who have faith in the promise as Abraham did when he believed God. A true Israelite, in New

Testament terms, is one who trusts in the promises of God fulfilled in Jesus, the Messiah of Israel. The Israel of the New Testament is the Church, not a specific people or parcel of land.

18. The "children of the slave woman" are those who live under the Law, particularly the law of Sinai. The "children of the free woman" are those who have been born from above from their free mother, the Church, a reference to Baptism. In Baptism we are conceived and born as children of the free woman, children of the promise.

Children of God (Connect)

19. The image of new birth and new creation is a strong one in John's Gospel. In this prologue, John sets the tone leading up to the incarnation. All who receive Christ, that is, believe in His name (trust His person and work), are given the right to become children of God. This is a new and heavenly birth—not born out of descent, decision, or by natural conception, but born of God. This birth is a new birth "from above" (the Greek word in 3:3 means both "again" and "from above"). It is a new creation by water and Spirit (see Genesis 1:2). The allusion is obviously to Baptism.

20. The text is better translated as "sons of God" even when referring to females. Inheritance is the point of comparison. All are equally heirs according to the promise fulfilled in Abraham's Seed (that is, Christ) whether they are Jew or Gentile by birth, slave or free in status, male or female. Note that this passage does not obliterate these distinctions but states that in Christ these distinctions have no validity. In this world, we continue to live in the various orderings into which God has placed us. The two gifts of Baptism in this passage are (1) that we are Abraham's offspring (even if we are not related by blood to Abraham) and (2) that we are heirs according to the promise. Women also are "sons" in the sense that they are coequal heirs of eternal life and are not connected to a father or husband for salvation.

A New You (Vision)

21. In spite of their sinful past, the Corinthians' identity comes from what God has done for them in Christ. They were washed (baptized), sanctified (made holy), and justified (declared righteous) in the name of Jesus and by the Holy Spirit. That is their identity over and against their past. Their future is that they will inherit eternal life,

even though those who commit such sins do not. Our baptismal identity causes us to identify with Christ rather than our sins and to disown our sins as not being "who we are" in Christ.

22. Paul's exhortation to holiness is not a command to shape up or ship out, but a call to be who we already are as God's children. God's children are "imitators of God," living lives of love, maintaining sexual purity, and edifying speech. As "children of light," they do not participate in the works of darkness but expose them for what they are. Instead of drunkenness, they are filled with the Spirit and address each other with psalms, hymns, and spiritual songs, giving thanks to the Father through the Son. Repentance and forgiveness is a continual call out of darkness into light, returning to our Baptism and our baptismal identity as God's children of the promise.

The Promise of Baptism

Objectives

By the power of the Holy Spirit working through God's Word, participants will (1) rejoice in their Baptism; (2) see the various ways in which God does wondrous things through water and His Word; (3) recognize that in Baptism the promises of God are applied personally to the individual; and (4) see Holy Baptism as the foundational act of God in their spiritual lives.

Opening Worship

Holy and most gracious heavenly Father in Holy Baptism You have made us your own children and have given us every spiritual blessing in Christ Jesus, our Savior. In the water with the Word You have made us a new creation in Christ and have united us with Him in His death, resurrection, and glory. Grant that each day we may die to sin and rise to new life in Jesus, that we would draw deeply from the wells of salvation and be refreshed in our journey until we come to the promised land of the resurrection; through Jesus Christ, our Lord. Amen.

Psalm: Psalm 51
Sing "All Christians Who Have Been Baptized" (*LSB* 596).

Focus

23. The purpose of this question is to draw the participants into a discussion about their own baptismal identity. Expressions will, of course, vary. Some may even see Luther's statement as a license to sin using Baptism as a cover.

Through Water and Spirit (Inform)

24. According to the account of the creation in Genesis 1, the earth was covered with water and the Spirit of God hovered over the waters. What follows is a sequence of God's speaking into the cre-

ation to call forth life and bring order out of chaos. All life has its basis in "water and Spirit with the Word" according to Genesis.

25. The flood returned the earth to its state in Genesis 1:2. In this sense, the flood was a type of baptism of the earth, a death of the creation and most of the world's inhabitants, and a resurrection of Noah and the representatives of the creation kept in safety in the ark. Curiously, the ark was first opened on Noah's 601st birthday! It was a kind of new birth for Noah and those under him. Peter links the flood and the ark to Baptism, "which now saves you." The promise in Baptism in 1 Peter 3 is that of a clear conscience before God through the resurrection of Jesus.

26. The crossing of the Red Sea was Israel's birth as a nation and the drowning of Israel's enemy, the army of Pharaoh. Notice that a great east wind blew across the Sea as it parted (Exodus 14:21). The Hebrew word for *spirit* and *wind* are the same, as is also *breath.* At Pentecost, the Holy Spirit was manifested as a rushing wind—Acts 2. In crossing the parted sea, Israel emerged as God's own people (compare Exodus 19:6 and 1 Peter 2:9), baptized into Moses (1 Corinthians 10:2).

27. Through the prophet Elisha, God spoke His promise of physical healing to Naaman. The actual healing took place when Naaman entered the waters of the Jordan. The text notes that the healing was so extensive or significant that Naaman's skin was renewed like that of a young boy. So, in a sense, God's healing of Naaman served like a physical "rebirth."

28. The Father openly declared Jesus to be His beloved Son (compare with Isaiah 42:1 and the "servant of Yahweh"). The Holy Spirit descended visibly in the form of a dove. As Jesus told John, who had objected to the arrangement, "It is proper for us to do this in order to fulfill all righteousness." In His Baptism, Jesus identified Himself with us sinners, so that in our Baptism we might receive His righteousness (see 2 Corinthians 5:21).

29. The only imperative in this passage is "make disciples" or "disciple the nations." Disciples are made by baptizing in the triune name of God and teaching them everything Christ has mandated. There is no temporal sequence implied in the text. One can be baptized into teaching or taught into Baptism; either way, the result is the same—a disciple. Jesus promises to be with them in this "discipling" activity until the end of the age. When they baptized, He is the One who is baptizing; when they teach, He is the Teacher. The disciples, as ministers, are His instruments.

For You and for Your Children (Connect)

30. Peter promises the forgiveness of sins and the Holy Spirit. The promise, he says, is not only to those who are there to hear it but also to their children, literally whomever God calls, whether far or near. Similarly, Paul applied the promise of Baptism to the Philippian jailer and his entire household, which would have included not only his own children but also his servants and their children. The promise of Baptism applied to children is nothing else than to say that (1) children are born in sin and in need of salvation, and (2) Jesus died for all—including children. There are no limits to the Gospel, including age limits.

31. Baptism buries us with Christ in His death. Since children are born into the sin and death of Adam, which is proven by the fact that they can die, it would make sense that they should be united with Christ in His death and life as soon as possible. Parents would want the greatest possible confidence that their child is in Christ and therefore a child of the promise. This is not to say that those who are not baptized cannot be saved, but God gives us the gift of Baptism for the certainty of salvation in Christ.

The Promises Overflow (Vision)

32. Mark 16:16—salvation to those who believe and are baptized

Galatians 3:27—clothed in Christ (Note: It is better to translate this in the passive rather than the reflexive. "For as many of you as were baptized into Christ have been clothed with Christ." The white robe sometimes given to the newly baptized in the rite of Baptism is symbolic of being clothed with Christ.)

Colossians 2:12—burial and resurrection in Christ

1 Peter 3:21—salvation

Titus 3:5—rebirth and renewal by the Holy Spirit

33. A seal (Greek: *sphragis*) is a mark of ownership. Soldiers in Caesar's army received such a mark on their foreheads to show their allegiance to Caesar. In Revelation 7 (based on Ezekiel 9), those who are marked by the Lamb are safe from the destruction of the final judgment. In placing His mark of ownership on us, God is making a promise that we belong to Him. In Ephesians 1:13, this is seen as a down payment or guarantee of our redemption and the inheritance of eternal life.

The Promise of Absolution

Objectives

By the power of the Holy Spirit working through God's Word, participants will (1) treasure the gift of Holy Absolution and its promises; (2) see Holy Absolution as a return to Baptism and a cleansing by the Word of God; (3) utilize the blessings of Absolution in their own lives and in their dealings with others; and (4) see forgiveness as a central blessing in their spiritual lives.

Opening Worship

Holy and gracious God our heavenly Father, Your Son died and rose to win forgiveness of all of humanity, and He has ordained that forgiveness be spoken and heard in His name. Grant us to know ever more deeply the boundless depths of your mercy in Jesus, be cleansed by Your Word, and live our lives before You and those around us as Your forgiven children; hear us for Jesus' sake, Amen.

Psalm: 32
Sing " 'As Surely as I Live,' God Said" (*LSB* 614; *ELH* 417; *CW* 308; *LW* 235; *TLH* 331).

Focus

34. Responses will vary. The purpose of these questions is to have the participants discuss the experience of forgiving and being forgiven and how guilt and shame are prisons that bind us and separate us from each other.

A Cleansing Word (Inform)

35. David himself pronounced his own sentence by saying, "This man deserves to die." Nathan turned the tables on David by saying, "You are the man." In spite of all that the Lord had given to David, David had taken another man's wife as his own and killed her husband. In doing so, he had despised the Lord Himself. David con-

fesses that he has "sinned against the Lord." All sin, no matter how great or small, is a sin against God. Nathan speaks a word of forgiveness to David—"The Lord has taken away your sin." Nevertheless, God still imposes a discipline. The son born to David by Bathsheba will die. David is forgiven but he is still disciplined by the Lord, as we all are. Though God forgives, and we do not die as sinners, He nevertheless imposes temporal disciplines to teach and admonish us and others (see Hebrews 12:5<en>11).

36. David's son died on the seventh day, one day short of his circumcision, which would have occurred on the eighth day. The child dies without circumcision or name. David indicates that he will go to his son one day, and he breaks his fast and worships the Lord. God remembers the promise he once made to David through Nathan and gives him a son, Solomon, by Bathsheba. Solomon succeeded David in office as king and was an ancestor of Jesus.

37. The disciples were afraid of the Jews. Jesus had been arrested and crucified, and they feared they were next. Jesus appears visibly to show His wounds His hands and side and to speak words of peace—"Peace be with you." Jesus' words always give what they say. With His breath and His words, Jesus gives the Holy Spirit to His disciples and sends them as apostles and ministers with the authority to forgive sins. With the same Spirit and words, we hear the words of forgiveness from Christ through His authorized representatives in the Office of the Holy Ministry, trusting that we are hearing forgiveness from the Lord Himself. Pastors extend God's forgiveness in Christ on behalf of the Church. However, Absolution is the prerogative of every Christian.

38. When someone sins against us, we are to go to that person alone; then take one or two others as witnesses; and finally, when all else fails, we are to bring the matter to the whole congregation. Every avenue for forgiveness and reconciliation is used. Within that community of believers, there is the authority to bind and loose, to free people from the chains of sin, guilt, and shame and bring them into the freedom of forgiveness. Luther called the Church a "mouth-house of forgiveness," that is, a place where forgiveness is spoken. This is the true and proper work of the Church, as it says in the small catechism, to "daily and richly forgive sins to me and all believers."

39. The psalmist David speaks of his bones wasting away and his strength being sapped as on a hot day. He feels the heavy hand of the Lord upon him. There are physical as well as spiritual effects to sin. The silence is literally killing him. In confessing his sin, David

finds release. God forgives the guilt of his sin. Instead of wasting his energy covering up his sin, David is now free to rejoice and be glad and sing, as well as teach others in the way they should go. In James 5, the sick are ministered to with prayer, anointing, and also confession in the same recognition that what is good for the soul is also good for the body.

40. It is not clear whether the man is the one excommunicated in 1 Corinthians 5 or a different one. Regardless, he has repented and desires to be readmitted, and Paul encourages the congregation to reach out to him. Paul does not desire that he be overwhelmed by excessive sorrow. The ultimate goal of any church discipline is the repentance and restoration of the sinner to the life of forgiveness.

Joy Restored (Connect)

41. Psalm 51 is traditionally ascribed to David when the prophet Nathan confronted him with his adultery and murder. David confesses that he has sinned against the Lord and has done "what is evil in Your sight." Sin always has a vertical component; it is always before the Lord. David recognizes that sin has been his condition from the very moment of his own conception. Even the developing child in the womb is sinful in the sense that he or she is conceived in the same hereditary guilt from Adam. We sin because we are sinful; the sins that we do are the result of our sinful condition. This is why even a tiny baby who is not capable of much action or speech is still considered sinful. It is a condition of natural-born man.

42. Sin always robs us of joy whether in our wallowing in guilt and shame, our hiding from others, or our anxiety over getting caught. In fact, getting caught is the first step toward freedom. The silence of the secret has been broken, and now a word of forgiveness can be spoken and heard. Having been forgiven, David is now in a position to teach others as well, and also to worship, that is, to offer right sacrifices. As long as we are bound up in sin, we will attempt to justify ourselves and futilely try to atone for our sins. Such sacrifices God does not desire. He desires instead broken and contrite hearts. Having been forgiven and set free, we are then in a position to offer right and pleasing thank offerings to God.

An Embassy of Reconciliation (Vision)

43. Those who are "in Christ" have already died and have become a "new creation," the old is gone and the new has come. The certainty that we are "in Christ" comes not from within us, but from God in our Baptism and in the word of forgiveness (Absolution) that restores us (see Ephesians 1:13–14). In the death of Christ, God the Father reconciled the world to Himself, which means that in Christ He no longer counts people's sins against them. They are justified in Jesus. Jesus took on humanity's sin in His innocence, so that we might receive His righteousness as a gift. This is what Luther called a "sweet swap"—our sin for Jesus' righteousness.

44. Forgiveness is without limits or boundaries. The first servant is forgiven much by the king, an outrageous debt. The second servant is forgiven little, a petty debt. Jesus amplifies the difference to remind us of how great God's forgiveness is to each of us. When we forgive each other, we are drawing upon the infinite resource of God's forgiveness in Jesus. Therefore, there can be no limits to forgiveness, whether by the congregation or by the individual. Refusal to forgive implies limits on God's forgiveness and is a denial of the atoning sacrifice of Jesus. The Christian and the Christian congregation will always look for opportunities to forgive and restore the sinner to a right relationship with God and with each other.

The Promise of the Lord's Supper

Objectives

By the power of the Holy Spirit working through God's Word, participants will (1) see the Lord's Supper in the greater biblical context of table fellowship with God; (2) develop a magnified hunger and thirst for the Sacraments; (3) see the centrality of the Lord's Supper in the spiritual life of the Christian; and (4) partake of the Sacrament with knowledge and intentionally.

Opening Worship

Holy and most gracious Father, on the night He was betrayed into death, our Lord Jesus Christ gave His body and blood for His own disciples to eat and drink that they might remember His sacrifice and cling to Him in faith. Stir up in us, we pray, a hunger and thirst for this gift, that we might remember our Savior and abide in Him as He also abides in us; through Jesus Christ, our Lord. Amen.

Psalm: Psalm 116
Sing "O Lord, We Praise Thee" (*LSB* 617; *ELH* 327; *CW* 317; *LW* 238; *LBW* 215; *TLH* 313).

Focus

45. The purpose of these questions is for the participants to discuss the place of the Lord's Supper in their spiritual lives. Responses will vary. Participants should be allowed to talk freely about the Lord's Supper as it pertains to their own life of faith.

Eating and Drinking with God (Inform)

46. For centuries and generations following, every Israelite family participated in the Passover in communion with all Israel. At the

Passover table, children learned from their fathers as they told the narrative of God's deliverance. In taking the bread and cup of the Passover, Jesus did something new with it. Yet it is connected in a deep way. In the Lord's Supper, we are united with Christ in His exodus through death to life and also with one another as fellow Israelites of the new covenant in Christ's shed blood.

47. Moses sprinkled the blood on the people with the words, "This is the blood of the covenant." As sure as the blood landed on someone and stained his or her robe, so sure was he or she that he or she was in the covenant. The Israelites heard the Word of God and the blood of the covenant. Moses and Aaron, Nadab and Abihu, and the seventy elders of Israel ate and drank with God on His mountain. Though no one may see God and live to tell about it, these men ate and drank in God's presence and were not harmed. In the same way, we eat and drink in the presence of God at the Lord's Supper, and Christ gives us forgiveness, life, and salvation with the body and blood along with His words.

48. Elijah was sustained in his wilderness journey by bread and water supplied by an angel. This hearkened back to Israel being sustained by bread (manna) and water in the wilderness. The angel tells Elijah that the journey is too long and arduous for him without this food and drink. In the same way, our life of faith is too long and demanding without the sustenance of Jesus' body and blood. Notice that the strength of the food God gave him, Elijah was able to complete the forty-day trek to Sinai.

49. In John 6, Jesus preaches a sermon in the Capernaum synagogue that outraged even His own disciples. He begins by calling Himself the "living bread" and saying that He is greater than Moses and the manna eaten by Israel. To believe in Jesus is to eat of this "living bread" that came down from heaven. As He continues, Jesus intensifies the eating of Him by faith to a scandalous eating of Him with the mouth. While Jesus is not speaking directly on the Lord's Supper as He does in the words of institution, nevertheless, His words are clearly an allusion to the Lord's Supper just as His words in John 3:5 are a clear allusion to Baptism. In John 6, Jesus promises that those who believe in Him and who eat His flesh and drink His blood have life in them, and He will raise them up on the Last Day. When we read this account and the question of the outraged hearers in the Capernaum synagogue, we know the answer. How can this man give us His flesh to eat and His blood to drink? In the bread and wine of the Lord's Supper, of course!

50. Each account provides some unique details. Matthew mentions that it is for the "forgiveness of sins." Matthew and Mark emphasize the blood in the cup while Luke accents the "new covenant." Luke also has the command "Do this in remembrance of Me." Luke also gives us more details concerning the Passover meal. The cup of the Lord's Supper is the "cup of blessing" (1 Corinthians 10:16), the third cup of the Passover meal, which immediately followed the supper. Luke mentions also a cup before the meal began.

51. The account in 1 Corinthians is an account of the Lord's Supper given to Paul "from the Lord." It reflects the ongoing nature of the Lord's Supper as a liturgical act in the Church. There is a mandate to "Do this" both for the bread and for the cup. Paul also specifies that this is to continue until the Lord comes, that is, until the Last Day (1 Corinthians 11:26). This account provides the confidence that the Lord intended this meal to continue in His Church until the end of days. It also demonstrates the centrality of the Lord's Supper in the life of the Church. In addition, Paul provides some instructions concerning the right use of the holy Supper in verses 27–32.

The Breaking of the Bread (Connect)

52. In Jesus' encounter with the two disciples on the Emmaus road, He first taught them from the Scriptures (the Old Testament) about His suffering, death, and resurrection, and then revealed Himself in the house in the breaking of the bread. It was a "Word and Sacrament" event. Jesus teaches that the main point of the Scriptures is Himself—His death and resurrection. Though the disciples were prevented from recognizing Jesus (it wasn't their fault), He revealed Himself as He broke the bread at the table. The story indicates that Jesus would be present in His Church in a new way from now on; not visibly and locally as the disciples had experienced Him, but He would be recognized in the "breaking of the bread," that is, in His Supper.

53. The first believers gathered daily in the temple for the morning and evening offices of prayer. They also gathered in private homes to celebrate the Lord's Supper in fellowship with one another. As a fellowship, they had all their possessions in common. Luke tells us that they were devoted to the doctrine of the apostles, the communion or fellowship, which is the "breaking of the bread," and to the prayers. (The syntax of this sentence in the Greek text favors three distinct elements to four—doctrine, communion, prayer.) This is the

outline of the Divine Service as we know it—the service of the Word, in which the doctrine of the apostles is preached, and the service of the Sacrament, in which the Lord Jesus makes Himself known to us in the breaking of the bread.

One Bread, One Body (Vision)

54. The apostle Paul states that we are one body because we eat of one bread. We also drink of one blood. Since the same body and blood are given to and received by all communicants, we share or have these things in common. This is what the word *communion* or *fellowship* means—to have something in common. In the Sacrament, our unity in Christ is revealed and manifested. Therefore, it is vitally important that there be no divisions among us (as there were in Corinth and against which Paul warned). Our communion is not only with Christ, but it is also with one another as the body of Christ.

55. The members of the Corinthian congregation were getting drunk at their fellowship meal and despising the poor and hungry among their own members. Both of these things were denials of their unity in Christ. In failing to discern the body of the Lord in the Supper and their unity together as the body of Christ, they incurred God's temporal judgment—some became ill and some even died. To avoid this, Paul says that they are to examine themselves in light of the gift that is being given and, in this way, eat of the bread and drink of the cup.

The greeting of peace is an ancient sign of our peace and reconciliation in Christ. The symbol has varied. In the Church it was a kiss. Later, everyone kissed a cross. Today, in our culture, it is a handshake and verbal greeting. All of these things show our unity in the body of Christ. Luther's 1526 post-Communion prayer asks that the gifts received would work faith toward God and love toward the neighbor. Faith and love were the two ways that a Christian lived outside of himself or herself. This is precisely what is lacking in the Corinthian congregation—faith and love. These two are also inseparable—there can be no faith in Christ without love for the neighbor; there can be no fully God-pleasing love for the neighbor without faith in Christ.

The Promise of Life

Objectives

By the power of the Holy Spirit working through God's Word, participants will (1) recognize that the promises of God in Christ are a promise for life in Christ; (2) see that the abundant life Jesus promises is a life in communion with Him in His Church; (3) realize that life in Christ is also fruitful life; and (4) look forward with joy and hope to the fulfillment of God's promises in Christ in the resurrection of the dead and the life of the world to come.

Opening Worship

Gracious God, our Father in heaven, You have given us rich promises of life in abundance in Your Son, our Savior Jesus Christ. By His death and resurrection, You have brought humanity out of captivity to death and into the life of the new creation. In our Baptism, You have given us life in Jesus and the hope of yet greater blessing in the life to come. Grant that we would daily rejoice in our life in Christ, reflect it to the world around us, lead others to know the life that is theirs in Jesus, and finally, by Your grace in Christ, attain to the promised inheritance of life everlasting; through Jesus Christ, our Lord. Amen.

Psalm: Psalm 27
Sing "O God, O Lord of Heaven and Earth" (*LSB* 834; *CW* 400; *LW* 319; *LBW* 396).

Focus

56. The purpose of these questions is to help participants explore the implications of eternal life in their present lives. The leader will want to try and expand the idea of "life" beyond the usual concerns.

Abundant Life (Inform)

57. The Good Shepherd gives life to His sheep. He protects them from robbers and wolves; they recognize His voice and follow Him; He lays down His life for the sheep. When read in this context, Psalm 23 provides a wonderful job description of the Good Shepherd: He leads the sheep to quiet waters and green pasture; He restores them when they fall down; He leads them through the threatening dark valley of death, going before them; He anoints their wounds with oil; He prepares a feast for them in the presence of their enemies. Good Shepherd Jesus leads us through death to resurrection, having gone the way ahead of us. He baptizes us in the quiet waters of Baptism; He anoints us with the healing balm of forgiveness in Absolution; He grants us a place at His table where He feeds us His own body and blood in the presence of our enemies: sin, death, devil, our sinful nature, and the Law that condemns us.

58. Jesus is to the believer as the vine is to the branch. The branch draws its life from the vine and is nourished by it. We abide in Christ, and Christ abides in us; His life is our life, and His life is fruitful. The Father "prunes" (disciplines) us not to punish us as our sins deserve but that we might be even more fruitful. This pruning occurs in the day-to-day encounter with God's Law that kills us in order that we may be raised to life in Christ. Jesus promises that we will receive whatever we ask, provided that we abide in Him through faith and He abides in us through His Word. This is not a *carte blanche* promising the affirmative answer to every prayer but the promise that, as the life of Christ flows through us, our will and Christ's will are one so that our requests are shaped to His will. In the Lord's Supper, the death and life of Christ literally flow into us as His body and blood. It is no accident that illustration of the vine was used in the Upper Room on the night Jesus was betrayed and instituted the Lord's Supper!

The church father Cyril of Alexandria wrote this: "For who has doubted that Christ is in this manner a vine, and we the branches, deriving life for ourselves from this? Hear Paul saying, "For you are all one in Christ Jesus; so we, though many, are one body in Christ; for we all partake of the one bread" (Galatians 3:28; Romans 12:5; 1 Corinthians 10:17). Does he perhaps think that the virtue of the mystical benediction is unknown to us? Since this is in us, does it not also, by the communication of Christ's flesh, cause Christ to dwell in us bodily?" (Apology of the Augsburg Confession, Article X, paragraph 56).

59. Neither the birds nor the lilies are anxious for anything in their lives, yet God provides abundantly for them. We are worth the price of God's Son, Jesus, and His holy, precious blood shed on the cross for our redemption. By worrying, we are deprived of rest and often fail to see what God has already provided us without our asking. In Philippians 4, Paul states that the antidote for anxiety is prayer with thanksgiving. The phrase "with thanksgiving" indicates that we are to ask our petitions all the while thanking God for the circumstances and need that brought us to prayer in the first place. (Remember, Paul was in prison when he wrote the joyful Letter to the Philippians!) The promise of prayer is not that we will get whatever we ask for, but that the peace of God that surpasses our understanding will keep our hearts and minds where they belong and where our life is—in Christ Jesus, our Lord.

60. Jesus promises the Holy Spirit to His disciples. He is "another Helper." In sending the Spirit from the Father, Jesus Himself will be with His disciples so that they will never be alone in this life. The spiritual life is life in the Holy Spirit. His work is to convict and convince the world of sin, righteousness, and judgment. He is the "UPS delivery man" of the Trinity, taking from what Jesus has and delivering it to us through the Word and Sacraments.

61. In the third part of His high priestly prayer, Jesus prays for all who would believe through the apostolic Word. That includes all believers, including us. He prays that they may be brought to complete unity in Him, just as He and the Father are one. This is not as some believe an external or institutional unity of the churches but our mystical, hidden union with Christ as our life is in Him. He prays also that we would be with Him and see His glory that He eternally has from the Father. This is Jesus' abiding prayer for us and for the whole Church. What a comfort to know that Jesus is continually interceding for us as our own High Priest and that we need no other mediator save Jesus.

62. The penitent thief prayed, "Jesus remember me, when You come into Your kingdom." He didn't pray to be saved or to be spared his cross; he recognized that his death sentence was well deserved but that Jesus was innocent of any wrongdoing. In turn, Jesus promised the dying thief paradise: "Today you will be with Me in Paradise." Paradise was another name for heaven in the vocabulary of Jesus' day. Even though the thief was about to die, his life was held safely in

the man dying next to him who promised him paradise. This is Jesus' promise to all who trust in Him as that thief did, a promise we can take to our deathbed: "Today you will be with Me in Paradise."

Now Heard, Not Yet Seen (Connect)

63. Ephesians 1:3–14 is a marvelous run-on sentence in Greek, emphasizing that one thing cannot be isolated from the next. At least ten times in this passage, Paul underscores the fact that all our spiritual blessings are in Christ. In Christ we are chosen, predestined, adopted, redeemed, and forgiven. The plan and purpose of God's eternal will is to unite (the Greek word means "recapitulate" or "bring together under one head") all things in heaven and earth in Christ. We were included in Christ when we first heard the Word of the Gospel and were baptized (marked) with the seal of the promised Holy Spirit, a deposit or guarantee of the fulfillment to come in the resurrection.

64. In Hebrews, faith is certainty in a promise, the things hoped for but not yet seen. The writer to the Hebrews gives a kind of hall of fame of the faithful. From faithful Abel to Enoch, Noah, Abraham, Isaac, Jacob, Joseph, Moses, Rahab, Gideon, David, and a host of others, we see how the faithful lived by faith and not by sight, trusting the promises of God over and against what they saw and experienced in their own lives. Their abundant life in Christ was lived in hopeful expectation of our union together with Him. The spiritual life of faith is one of hearing the Word of God and trusting in His promises, not in receiving and seeing the fulfillment of every promise in this life.

God's Last Promise, and His First (Vision)

65. The seven churches of Asia Minor to whom John was writing the account of this vision were real congregations living in an actual time in history. They also provide a cross section of the Church as it is throughout all time—faithful, conflicted, heterodox, complacent, poor, struggling. Yet to each of the churches there is a specific promise of life and salvation from Christ, the Lord of the Church. To doctrinally pure though loveless Ephesus—the right to eat from the tree of life. To poor and faithful Smryna—the crown of life. To steadfast though immoral Pergamum—a new name. To persevering though heterodox Thyatira—authority over the nations. To sleepy Sardis—unsoiled clothing and names not blotted out of the Book of Life. To weak but faithful Philadelphia—the name of God and of His

city. To complacent, lukewarm Laodicea—new clothes, salve for their eyes, and table fellowship with Christ.

66. As we have seen, water and Spirit always go together in the Scriptures (see John 3:5). The river of the water of life is a picture of the Holy Spirit flowing from the throne of God (the Father) and the Lamb (the Son) down the center of the city. The tree of life (Genesis 3:24) straddles the river (the Spirit is the Lord and Giver of life). It is once again accessible to the nations, now bearing fruit twelve months in the year, and its leaves are a healing medicine for the nations. What began in a garden ends in a glorious city with the tree of life in a kind of central park within the heavenly city of God. The promise of enmity with the devil has come to its fulfillment, and he who by a tree once overcame now has been overcome by the tree of the cross. The result is that we might once again eat from the tree of life and live forever. The final promise of Scripture is the fervent prayer of the Church as she lives in the watchful waiting of the end times. Jesus promises, "I am coming soon" (this can also be translated, "I come quickly"). And the Church prays, "Amen. Come, Lord Jesus."

This is the prayer of the spiritual life of the promise, a life of hopeful expectation, lived in the "now" of new life in Christ and in the hope of eternal life to come in the resurrection. Each and every day of a baptized believer's life is lived in the hope of this prayer: "Amen. Come, Lord Jesus."

Appendix of Lutheran Teaching

Below you will find examples of how the first Lutherans addressed the issues of faith and God's promises.

Justifying Faith Is Trust in the Promise

Faith means not only a knowledge of the history but the kind of faith that believes in the promise. Paul plainly testifies about this when he says in Romans 4:16, "That is why it depends on faith, in order that the promise may rest on grace and be guaranteed." He judges that the promise cannot be received unless it comes through faith. Therefore, he puts them together as things that belong to one another. He connects the promise and faith. It will be easy to decide what faith is if we consider the Creed, where this article certainly stands: the forgiveness of sins. It is not enough to believe that Christ was born, suffered, was raised again, unless we add also this article, which is the purpose of the history: the forgiveness of sins. To this article the rest must be referred, namely, that for Christ's sake, and not because of our merits, forgiveness of sins is given to us. For what need was there that Christ was given for our sins if our merits can make satisfaction for our sins? (Apology IV 50–52)

The Promise Must Always Be in View of Faith

The promise should always be in sight. Because of His promise, God wishes to be gracious and to justify for Christ's sake, not because of the Law or our works. In this promise timid consciences should seek reconciliation and justification. By this promise they should sustain themselves and be confident that they have a gracious God for Christ's sake, because of His promise. So works can never make a conscience peaceful. Only the promise can. If justification and peace of conscience must be sought in something other than love and works, then love and works do not justify. This is true even though they are virtues and belong to the righteousness of the Law, insofar as they are a fulfilling of the Law. Obedience to the Law justifies by the righteousness of the Law—if a person fulfills it. But imperfect righteousness of the Law is not accepted by God unless it is accepted because of faith. So legal righteousness does not justify, that is, it neither reconciles nor regenerates nor by itself makes us acceptable before God. (Apology V 59–60)

Justification Gained through Faith in the Promise

Since justification is gained through the free promise, it follows that we cannot justify ourselves. Otherwise, why would there be a need to promise? Since the promise can only be received by faith, the Gospel (which is properly the promise of forgiveness of sins and of justification for Christ's sake) proclaims the righteousness of faith in Christ. The Law does not teach this, nor is this the righteousness of the Law. For the Law demands our works and our perfection. But, for Christ's sake, the Gospel freely offers reconciliation to us, who have been vanquished by sin and death. This is received not by works, but by faith alone. This faith does not bring to God confidence in one's own merits, but only confidence in the promise, or the mercy promised in Christ. This special faith (by which an individual believes that for Christ's sake his sins are forgiven him, and that for Christ's sake God is reconciled and sees us favorably) gains forgiveness of sins and justifies us. In repentance, namely, in terrors, this faith comforts and encourages hearts. It regenerates us and brings the Holy Spirit so that we may be able to fulfill God's Law: to love God, truly fear God, truly be confident that God hears prayer, and obey God in all afflictions. This faith puts to death concupiscence and the like. So faith freely receives forgiveness of sins. It sets Christ, the Mediator and Atoning Sacrifice, against God's wrath. It does not present our merits or our love. This faith is the true knowledge of Christ and helps itself to the benefits of Christ. This faith regenerates hearts and comes before the fulfilling of the Law. Not a syllable exists about this faith in the teaching of our adversaries. Therefore, we find equal fault with the adversaries because (a) they teach only the righteousness of the Law, and (b) they do not teach the righteousness of the Gospel, which proclaims the righteousness of faith in Christ. (Apology IV 43–47)

The Promise of Baptism

Therefore, every Christian has enough in Baptism to learn and to do all his life. For he has always enough to do by believing firmly what Baptism promises and brings: victory over death and the devil [Romans 6:3–6], forgiveness of sin [Acts 2:38], God's grace [Titus 3:5–6], the entire Christ, and the Holy Spirit with His gifts [1 Corinthians 6:11]. In short, Baptism is so far beyond us that if timid nature could realize this, it might well doubt whether it could be true. Think about it. Imagine there was a doctor somewhere who understood the art of saving people from death or, even though they died, could restore them quickly to life so that they would afterward live forever. Oh, how the world would pour in money like snow and rain. No one could find access to him because of the throng of the rich! But here in Baptism there is freely brought to everyone's door such a treasure and medicine that it utterly destroys death and preserves all people alive. (Large Catechism IV 41–43)

The Promise of Absolution

Here you see that Baptism, both in its power and meaning, includes also the third Sacrament, which has been called repentance. It is really nothing other than Baptism. What else is repentance but a serious attack on the old man ‹, that his lusts be restrained,› and an entering into a new life? Therefore, if you live in repentance, you walk in Baptism. For Baptism not only illustrates such a new life, but also produces, begins, and exercises it. For in Baptism are given grace, the Spirit, and power to suppress the old man, so that the new man may come forth and become strong [Romans 6:3–6]. (Large Catechism IV 74–76)

The Promise of the Lord's Supper

Therefore also, it is useless talk when they say that Christ's body and blood are not given and shed for us in the Lord's Supper, so we could not have forgiveness of sins in the Sacrament. Although the work is done and the forgiveness of sins is secured by the cross [John 19:30], it cannot come to us in any other way than through the Word. How would we know about it otherwise, that such a thing was accomplished or was to be given to us, unless it were presented by preaching or the oral Word [Romans 10:17; 1 Corinthians 1:21]? How do they know about it? Or how can they receive and make the forgiveness their own, unless they lay hold of and believe the Scriptures and the Gospel? But now the entire Gospel and the article of the Creed—I believe in . . . the holy Christian Church, . . . the forgiveness of sins, and so on—are embodied by the Word in this Sacrament and presented to us. Why, then, should we let this treasure be torn from the Sacrament when the fanatics must confess that these are the very words we hear everywhere in the Gospel? They cannot say that these words in the Sacrament are of no use, just as they dare not say that the entire Gospel or God's Word, apart from the Sacrament, is of no use. (Large Catechism V 31–32)

Glossary

Absolution. The application of the forgiveness of sins in Christ by means of the spoken word.

antinomianism. The teaching that the Law has no place in Christian proclamation or in the life of the believer. This view was championed by John Agricola at the time of the Reformation. It was rejected by both Luther and the Lutheran Confessions as it ultimately turned the Gospel into a new law.

cafeterianism. An attempt to create one's own worldview by selecting, cafeteria-style, religious or moral concepts, ideas, and practices from a variety of sources. A person who attends a Christian church on Sunday while believing in reincarnation might be viewed as a "cafeterian," for example, since bodily resurrection and reincarnation are inherently incompatible.

Darwinism. An explanation for the existence and diversity of life on earth, attributed to Charles Darwin, which includes such concepts as evolution, natural selection ("survival of the fittest"), adaptation, and other concepts.

enthusiasts. A term used by Luther to refer to the radical spiritualists who believed that God came to them apart from the external instruments of Word and Sacrament.

faith. God-given trust in the promise of forgiveness, life, and salvation on account of Jesus' life, death, and resurrection.

fundamentalism. A movement in the late nineteenth and twentieth centuries that stressed the inspiration and inerrancy of the Bible over Darwinism and other aspects of Enlightenment thought.

Gospel reductionism. Using the Gospel to suggest considerable latitude in faith and life not explicitly detailed in the Gospel.

grace. The undeserved kindness of God to forgive and save the sinner for Jesus' sake.

heterodox. A mixture of truth and error. A church is said to be "heterodox" when it holds to the central truth of the Gospel yet teaches errors that contradict the Gospel.

humanism. A broad range of philosophies that emphasize human dignity and worth and recognize a common morality based on universal, rational human nature. Humanists who deny the possibility of any supernatural involvement in human affairs are sometimes called secular humanists.

incarnate. To be "enfleshed," referring to the Second Person of the Trinity becoming a human being in the womb of the Virgin Mary. "The Word became flesh and dwelt among us" (John 1:14).

justification. The act of God by which a sinner is declared righteous before Him not because of the sinner's works but because of Jesus' perfect life and death on the sinner's behalf.

modernism. A cultural movement emerging in the late 1800s and later emphasizing the inevitability of human achievement (especially through science and technology) and a positive view of human reason, particularly its ability to determine the truth.

mysticism. While mysticism itself is a broad form of spirituality with distinct nuances, it is best characterized by the movement to transcend or move above the earthly through inward experience.

***oratio, meditatio, tentatio*.** Prayer, meditation, and trial. Luther said that theologians (students of God's Word) are made by prayer, meditation, and the trial of life under the cross.

postmodernism. Refers to a cluster of themes that are somewhat interconnected in their opposition to the attempts to establish truthfulness, which characterized the period of modernity. The focus of postmodernism is characterized by pluralism and the rejection of claims to absolute truth.

rationalism. The Enlightenment movement that saw human reason as the ultimate criterion for reality.

reductionism. A modern concept focusing on the human ability to reduce complex ideas or things to simple or more fundamental ideas or things. Fundamentalism exhibits reductionism in its attempt to reduce the Christian faith to very few "key" concepts or teachings. Gospel reductionism makes a similar error by devaluing or outright rejecting God's Law in the life of the believer (see also **antinomianism**).

righteousness. God's perfection and holiness. The righteousness of the Christian is the righteousness of Jesus Christ applied through faith in Christ.

type. A person, place, or event in the Old Testament that prefigures or pictures the person and work of Christ or the Church in the New Testament.